I BELIEVE

Meditations on
The Ten Commandments
and the Apostles' Creed

Paintings and Introductions by
ANNEKE KAAI

Verses by
ANGELA TAYLOR

First published 1995
by The Paternoster Press, P.O. Box 300, Carlisle CA3 0QS, U.K.

01 00 99 98 97 96 95   7 6 5 4 3 2 1

British Library Cataloguing in Publication Data

Kaai, Anneke
 I Believe:Meditations on the Ten
 Commandments and the Apostles' Creed in
 Word and Picture
 I. Title II. Taylor, Angela
 759.2
        ISBN 0-85364-693-7

INTRODUCTION

'I Believe' features two series of twenty-four paintings,
twelve on the Ten Commandments and twelve on
the Creed or the Apostolic Confession of Faith.
I have visualised these well-known words, so often
part of the worship liturgy in many churches,
to present them to you afresh.

Further information about the paintings themselves appears on page 56.

The Ten Commandments

The Ten Commandments or the Ten Words were given by God to
Moses on Mount Sinai as the rules by which his people, Israel, would
live in perfect happiness. I have used twelve paintings, because the first
sets the context in which the Commandments were given, 'I am the
Lord your God who led you out of Egypt, out of the land of slavery'
(Exodus 20). In the last painting, I have included the New Testament
fulfilment in Christ. It is in gratitude to him alone that we now can live
by these Words.

This series is currently the property of Arie Brandwijk, Sliedrecht, the Netherlands.

The Creed

The Creed, a summary of the Christian faith in twelve Articles,
put together by the young church, has endured the test of time. From
these statements emanates a tremendous power, the power which I
have experienced as inspiration in making these works of art. It is my
hope that you, too, will share in this experience.

Acknowledgements

First, I thank my husband and children, Geran and Riegonda, for their enthusiastic
interest and part in my work. Second, I thank Angela Taylor for the accompanying
English poems. Then my thanks go to the photographer Dolf Hoving, for his hard work
in producing the slides from the original lithos: to the publishers, The Paternoster Press
in the UK, Boekencentrum BV in the Netherlands and Brunnen-Verlag in Switzerland,
and to Pieter Kwant of The Paternoster Press for the enthusiasm with which
he has encouraged the English and Swiss editions.

Anneke Kaai

May, 1995

I am not ashamed of the gospel, for it is the power of God for the salvation of everyone who believes.

Romans 1:16

The Ten Commandments

The Ten Commandments, in Hebrew literally 'The Ten Words', can be found in Exodus 20. They were given by God to Moses and the people of Israel on Mount Sinai. Originally written on two stone tablets, they were the rules of life for the people of Israel. They are central to the Old Testament, indeed to the whole Bible. The first four Commandments deal with our relationship to God, the last six with the way we behave towards our neighbour. Through these twelve paintings I have tried to show the universal relevance of the Ten Commandments.

'I am the Lord your God who brought you out of Egypt, where you were slaves'.

From brick clay and ashes
a slave people is swept
in the curl of power.

The departure, gold-weighed,
as blood slid down lintels,
cut away Egypt.

A separation
and redemption.
A rooting
in new land,
in new law.

This first painting was inspired by the introduction to the Ten Commandments.
At the foot of the painting we see Egypt with its Nile delta in black, symbolizing
the slavery experienced by God's people. The silvery outline represents God
leading them to the fertile promised land shown in green, the colour of life.

'Worship no God but me'.

This no-god,
stiff, flat figure,
cracks open,
throwing no shadow
on the I AM:

the jealous one
who has heard
the screaming
of a people.

The Lord God anticipates the danger of his people worshipping foreign gods.
They had been introduced to them in the land of Egypt. 'Foreign gods' cloud
our vision of the one true God. They seem to offer us freedom, but although
they may be painted gold on the surface, they are cracked and empty within.
They turn pale and break before the face of God. They bring no happiness.

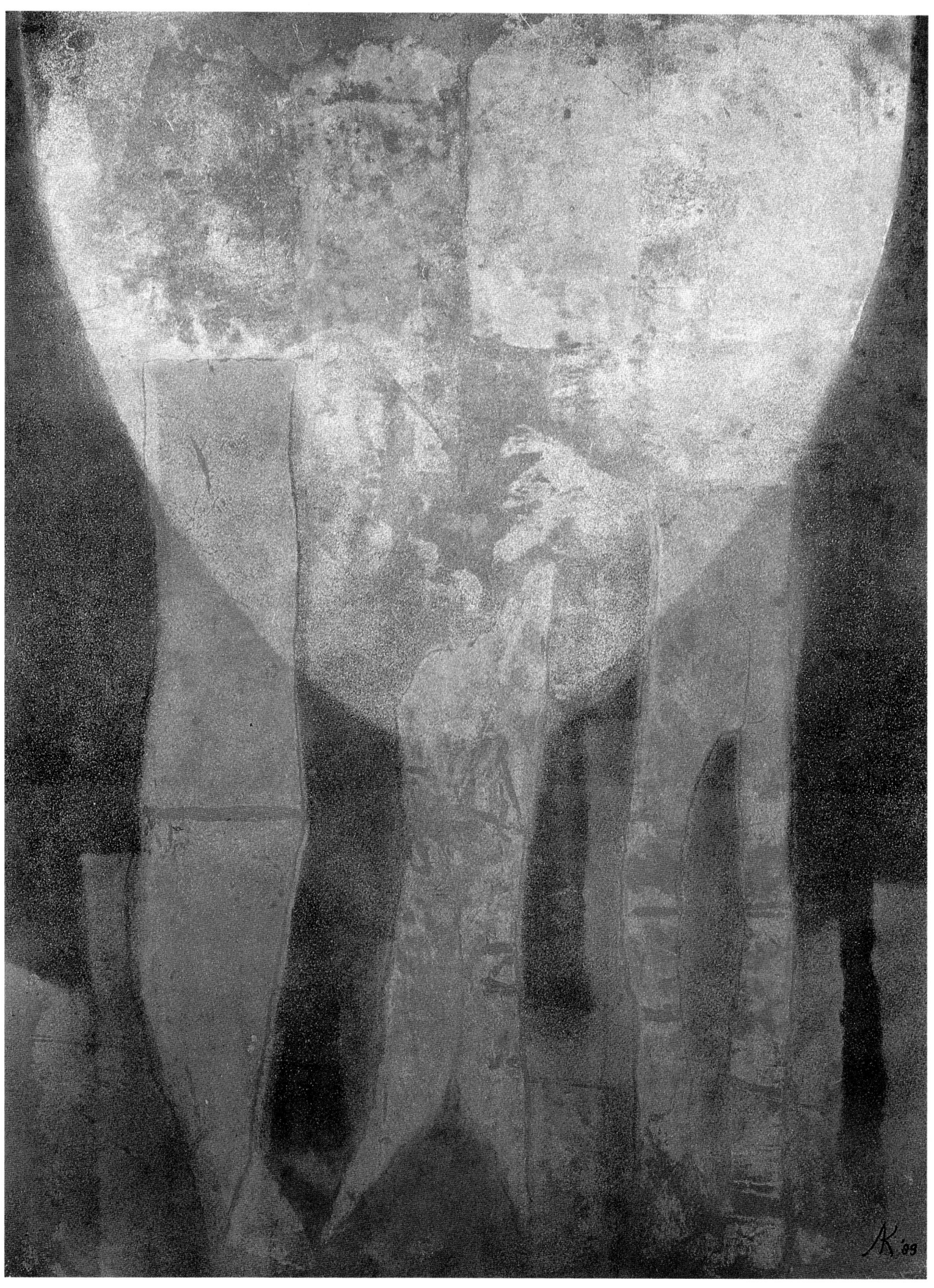

**'Do not make for yourself images of anything
in heaven or on earth or in the water
under the earth. Do not bow down
to any idol or worship it'.**

A crazed casting of gold
in mould of sand
and a calf is born,
bellowing against God,
from the smelting
of given wealth.

But in a powdered
and choking river
it swirls with no power:
lawless,
graceless.

This commandment is closely related to the first. Because God's people have
been in contact with so many idols, God forbids the making of any image for
the purpose of worship (the broken idol) of what is heaven (the light sphere)
or what lives on the earth, under the earth, or in the sea.

'Do not use my name for evil purposes'.

'This is the temple of the Lord,
the temple of the Lord,
the temple of the Lord...'

Words babble
and the name drips redly
from lips which do not taste.

In a night-scented garden
a crowd falls back.
'I am' shivers the air
where hang the tumbled letters
of his perjured character.

In the Bible a name indicates the bearer's character. This is also true of the Name of God, JHWH in Hebrew, which means 'I AM'. In the left-hand top corner of the painting we see this Name in a light plane. In the dark plane (the area of the powers of darkness) this name is jumbled up (Satan means over-thrower). The red colouring shows the danger of misusing God's Name.

'Observe the sabbath and keep it holy'.

Slaves scratched hot dirt,
for straw scraps.
Bricks, bricks, bricks.
Eyes earthward, nails cracked,
backs curved to hissing whips.

And on this one day,
with no manna to bake,
stillness hangs on families
unaccustomed to rest,
who eat yesterday's double gift.

God gave us six days to do all our work. In the painting these days are
shown equal in size. God tells us to keep one day holy, i.e. set apart.
We are to use this day specially to worship God in a spirit of peace
and quiet.

'Respect your father and mother'.

Desert walking,
the child hears
of a startling escape;
of wails for deaths,
but not his own;
of silver thrown in fear,
and walls of water.

Standing now on new ground,
each parent carries the Law
to their child,
who, bearing its weight,
honours the giver,
that the land might be free.

The Hebrew word for respect literally means 'making weighty'. We give
our parents the weight or importance due to them as the carriers of
the law they received from God. It should be passed on to their children
in turn. Blue dominates, symbolizing the faithfulness of God from
generation to generation.

'Do not commit murder'.

The skin was soft, mobile,
hands still sticky with sacrificial blood.
Corn seeds scattered
the wounded image of God,
first proof of the curse.
And a knife dripped in cramped fingers,
stunned by silence.

The knife twists,
buried in open flesh
and in the slashed canvas
of a name.
It is the cold eye meeting love,
a saving grasp
uncurling at the cliff's edge.

This commandment refers not only to physical killing (the long sword in the centre). We can also 'kill' our neighbour with the sword of the tongue (on the right of the painting), or through silence (the serpentine sword on the left), which can be as painful or worse than death by the other swords. We also see a sword to hasten death. We must sheathe all these swords in the soil to immobilize them. The dark spots on the soil (round shape) are a call to preserve the environment, so that the green of creation will again cover the whole earth.

'Do not commit adultery'.

The heat simmers round a glance,
at the wrong moment, from a roof top
and a killing, sadly, occurs,
in the van of battle.

Red blending of two
somehow is separated, rawly,
while a child sullenly cries
at a circle broken.
But he finds his experience
commonplace. It is yesterday's news.

A prophecy threatens
of fabrics frayed and unravelled.
There is no-one to honour.
There is no freedom.

Marriage, two together as one, complementing each other, is clearly
shown in this painting. God wants a husband and wife to maintain this
unity in marriage based on love (red) and faithfulness (blue shade).
Marriage also represents the relationship between Christ and the
church (interlocking cross and ring).

21

'Do not steal'.

A golden trench cuts the earth,
drinking wealth faster than

the stream of currency
raining heavily on the desert.

Somewhere, it is lost
in the steel of guns, or minds.

On the street, brogues scuff
a clamcase of coins.

Intrusive fingers at home
seek an elusive prize.

The wide golden path symbolizes the rich, and the narrow, sober path the
poor. All possessions are a gift from God (shown by the white area above).
In this commandment, God tells us not to take a possession from someone
else, as it will never really be ours. This is seen in the painting where the
stolen portion does not form a unity with the whole. The colours remain
separated, reinforced by a black line.

'Do not accuse anyone falsely'.

Like a tent on a formica table,
their faces gather with horror and delight.
'Did you hear...?'

The voices are quick and indistinct.
And while it may not be true,
mind patterns are made.

Behind tears, headlines hint at truth.
These are our judges,
destroying an image
with newsprinted hands.

We do not know what is real.
Foundations shift.

This commandment tells us to speak only the truth (the silhouette of the
mouth on the right). When we distort the truth, we turn it upside-down
(the black silhouette on the left). What comes out of the mouth must be
truthful (the wide area at the foot of the painting).

'Do not desire another man's wife...'

In cool earth pit, Achan's treasure
cries louder than victory,
Louder than wailing after the rout.

Voluptuous Babylonian tapestry,
wedge of gold, weights of silver:
devoted things, buried.

His red hands hide in the linen folds
while the clan shrinks away
and stones rasp in Israel's hands.

Rocks lift to break the limbs
that over-reached; the heart
that coveted is crushed.

We lust for what belongs to another because it seems so desirable to us
(gold) and are driven by a desire for more (the grasping hands).
Red represents the danger of these desires.

'Christ fulfils the law'.

To love God and your neighbour, completely,
is an exacting command,
accomplished only by blood, sweat

and two hands raised, grasping
the anger of Law: lifted above
shoulders bearing our names

and stone pages, carved
by justice and certain truth.
Not the least mark has been lost.

This last painting shows Christ as the fulfilment of the law. The cross
embraces the two stone tablets of the law, all in perfect unity. Christ did not
come to destroy the law but to fulfil it through his death. We are called
to follow Him gladly, therefore this painting radiates light!

The Creed

The Creed, the twelve Articles of Faith, the Apostolic Confession, three names for what summarized the faith of the young church. Confessed throughout the ages, never divided or replaced, it was inspired by God, an inspiration I experienced in making this series of twelve paintings. Through this work I hope to show the expressiveness of the Creed.

I believe in God the Father Almighty, Maker of heaven and earth.

My leaf-veined life,
frail structure in
his Spirit hand,
is weak fraction of
Word-breathed Earth
and untold heavens.
He is knowledge, presence, power.
The one God.

God as Father is to me the most important part of this first Article of Faith. This fatherhood is represented by his loving, embracing arms (the white rounded shape at the top of the painting). This shape is repeatedly used in the following paintings to communicate this basic idea. From the abstract right hand comes the strong force by which the heavens and the earth are created. In contrast to the small earth we see the greatness of God.

And in Jesus Christ his only Son our Lord.

His hand offers
aching love,
wound-service,
and behind, the Spirit hand of
the father holds out him:
Word of the Earth,
Lord of my freedom.
He is service and incarnation.
The pattern.

Jesus said: 'He who has seen me has seen the Father.' I have shown this
unity of Father and Son by letting the embracing arms of the Father run
into the supporting arms of the Son, the mediator between his Father
and man (see the earth).

Who was conceived by the Holy Spirit, born of the Virgin Mary.

In the triptych
a tiny dove
brushes
a woman's head
with painted wings.
An overshadowing.
A conception.
God is, and
is formed.

The purity of the Virgin Mary is clearly shown, as well as the overshadowing by the Holy Spirit who conceives the Holy One.

Suffered under Pontius Pilate.

The judge
breathed air
with Truth
and, twisting, mopped
pragmatic hands
to appease blood-chants
from the crowd.
The suffering is
the folly and
the mystery.

Not only the detail of the crown of thorns and the blood show us the acute
suffering of Jesus, but also the large grey-black area which expresses his
utter loneliness and forsakenness.

Was crucified, dead and buried.
He descended into hell.

Crucified. Dead. Buried.
The Prince of this World
stamps seals on the
rock of the tomb,
shuttering the window of
a borrowed room.
There, he had left peace
for such a time.

Blackness covers the
face of the earth.
God is dead.

In this painting I have again strengthened the composition with a high
horizon to show the depth of suffering. We are reminded here of the
experience behind the exclamation: 'My God, my God why have you
forsaken me? I have been trampled underfoot like a worm' (Psalm 22).

41

On the third day He rose from the dead. He ascended into heaven, And sits at the right hand of God the Father Almighty.

Gowns flap.
Jars of spice clink dully
in the grief
of a damp dawn.
A weight of stone
is to be moved.

Waiting, casually, it might seem,
a messenger:
'Not here. Gone.'
The words are blunt.
They plead for the dead,
and turning,
meet the gardener,
His footsteps crushing
scent from the new earth.

Out of the depth of his suffering (black area) by the power of his
resurrection, Jesus now sits at the right hand of his Father
(the light area). The stone rolls away as a result of the
dynamic resurrection.

From thence He shall come to judge the quick and the dead.

Sweating in a humid June,
two labourers,
building a road,
share a drink,
family news:
births, deaths.
And as a cloud
covers the sun

one is gone.

On that day it will be better for Sodom and Gomorrah...

The earth erupts at
the explosion of trumpets
spewing out filth
and purity.

It is appointed once to die,

and then to stare
at the joy and horror:
choices realised.

The light and the dark figures show the living and the dead. In the background the new earth with its new life (the light green colour) in contrast with the old (the dark side on the right).

I believe in the Holy Spirit.

We heard crowds below, from the hot, packed room,
where we waited, scared, after death. The door,
we locked. It seemed, at first, a trick of light,
air through unglazed windows. Then flames sprang.

Power licked about heads, sparked in dark eyes.
In strength we burst the door, bounded stairs:
the nations would hear, would flood with the Word.
Impressed by God's seal, we saw the promise come.

By the Spirit you are carried along and set on fire (the flames)
to become a witness for the cross and the resurrection.

I believe in the holy catholic church, the communion of saints.

A hedged people, set apart, meeting
under the fish, entombed by joy or.... lonely,
praying for strength to crack open the door
kept locked. In blazing light or near darkness.
Or...headline hitting growth, noted impact.
All harvested as history snaps closed:
the world-time body in one chain
under each test triumphant, the battle complete.

The embracing cross of Christ and the supporting love of God (the light
rounded shape at the foot) are central. Surrounding the cross is the church,
despite its divisions (torn shapes) one in Christ, experiencing community
through baptism (blue for water) and the Lord's Supper
(red for Christ's blood).

I believe in the forgiveness of sins.

Handprints bruised the head of the lot-picked goat
pointed at sand, heat hazing the desert's
edge, an endless, a solitary place.
In the prints, was engrained Israel's sin.

The writing in the sand remained some hours,
there being little wind after they had
slipped away. 'Neither do I condemn you,'
he said, each word a hammered nail in flesh.

The red-black area represents sin. This contrasts with the visible part of the
cross, showing that Christ, through the cross, covers sin with his shed blood.

I believe in the resurrection of the body.

The body there, breathing
before the locked door,
was to be read.
Purpled scars punctuated the skin,
and fingers of one hand
brushed the rough lips
of a wound:

the first sheaf,
cut from the earth,
wrested from the tomb.

Each reunion
a foretaste of
the resurrection.

Here I show the resurrection of the natural body as a glorified body.
As a bud turns towards the light, so it will be at the resurrection.

I believe in the life everlasting.

Hoisted by gifted belief
we cross from death to
life in fullness; the crevass
traversed by the Son,
securing our adoption.

We live as in a glass, darkly,
looking for eternity begun,
striving for the unshakeable kingdom
that will, burning, come.

'This is eternal life, that they know You'. The light-path begins here on
earth. There is no end to it as it disappears over the horizon and runs into
the light green of the new earth. This path also represents the Father's
embracing arm. Everlasting life is forever in his care!

The Paintings

The series on the Ten Commandments, paintings all measuring 60 x 80cm, was produced by the mixed technique on a base of oil on perspex. Started in 1989, they were completed in 1990; but not in any particular order.

The series on the Apostles' Creed (70 x 100cm) was produced by the same technique. This series was started in 1990 and completed in 1992.

In the works on the Ten Commandments the stylized technique gives a formal effect which is in line with the Commandments themselves; but in contrast with the dynamism of the Creed. These dynamics are seen in the movement which characterizes these paintings. In both series an important role is played by the texture of the paint itself.

The works are not exuberant in colour; but where exuberance is necessary, it has not been avoided. The colours have been chosen for their symbolic power.

Anneke Kaai, née van Wijngaarden, was born in Naarden on 5 February 1951. She received her training at the Gooise Academie voor Beelende Kunsten, continuing her studies at the Gerrit Rietveld Academie in Amsterdam.

Inspired by the Bible and her faith, Anneke's work can be described as semi-abstract, and embraces much Christian symbolism. In addition to the series in this volume, she has painted sequences on the Creation (15 paintings), and Revelation (24, and visually realistic) as well as a large work on the Lord's Prayer. At present she is completing a series on the Psalms, with 12 paintings finished to date. She has published *Apocalypse* (1992) and, in Dutch, *Openbaring in Beeld* (1990/1992) and *De Schepping in Beeld* (1991).

Angela Taylor was born in the East Midlands and studied at Aberystwyth and Cambridge. After some time spent working amongst people with mental handicaps, she became a secondary school teacher. She and her husband, Jim, live in Cambridge.